"We have a limited number of days to live in this world. We can choose how to live each day. How will you live yours?"

Christopher Terry

Pivotal Road

Life Skills for Teens

START YOUR JOURNEY

By

Christopher Terry

Illustration & Cover Design by Megan Terry-Alvarez

Copyright 2023

Front Cover Homage

The Acacia Tree

The acacia tree is often one of unassuming and often overlooked tree species in the world. However, upon closer look, it is one of the most historically and biblically significant trees. In Exodus, we see acacia specifically used as the tabernacle for the Ark of the Covenant due to the wood's durability and natural resistance to the elements. It is from this usage that the acacia wood has become a symbol of perseverance, regeneration, and integrity; it denotes the immortality of the human soul, and is a reminder that when all seems lost, there is hope for a brighter tomorrow. – *Author Megan Terry-Alvarez*

My hope is that the following pages, like the magnificent Acacia Tree, will mark the beginning of your journey to weather the storm and overcome whatever difficulties you may face in pursuit of a better, everlasting tomorrow.

Acknowledgements

First and foremost, I want to acknowledge that none of this was possible without the grace and inspiration from God for placing this desire upon my heart to share my experiences from life to help others by creating "Pivotal Road". Secondly, I am sincerely grateful for the encouragement and support from my family, all of them, especially my children – Cameron, Megan and Nicole. The love I have for you is beyond words to describe how I feel and what you mean to me. I am humbled, honored and proud to be your dad. And to my loving, caring, thoughtful and selfless wife, Pam…you, me, together, forever, always, and before God…Amen.

Additionally, I want to extend a very special thank you to all the ministry teams and educational organizations that provided the opportunities, training, support and experiences in working with teens from all backgrounds that provided the foundation behind this program: Chino Valley Christian Church – Chino, CA; Saddleback Church – Lake Forest & San Juan Capistrano, CA Campuses; New Hope Church & Students Ministry – Durham, NC; Temple City Church – Selma, NC; Apple Valley Unified School District – Apple Valley, CA; Chino Valley Unified School District – Chino, CA; Saddleback Valley Unified School District – Mission Viejo, CA; the team at Vulnerable Children Ministries; Hope International University (formerly Pacific Christian College) and Champman University.

Forward

"Live Life to the Fullest and Be Inspired!" – Christopher Terry

I was introduced to life at a very early age when I became a product of divorced parents. In fact, everyone in my family has been divorced. Eventually, both my parents remarried, which set the stage for some unique experiences in family dynamics and dysfunctions. It also put me on a life journey that involved some tremendous experiences, relationships and household environments. The experiences created a lot of insecurities and confusion in trying to figure out who I was supposed to be and what was my purpose in life.

After my parents divorce, the twists and turns of life took off – good and bad. My mom kept me and my siblings active in sports and music throughout school. It was tough for her as a single parent raising four kids and living with my grandmother. Looking back, I still don't know how she managed except through love and sacrifice. What it did offer me was exposure to learning to adjust to different circumstances and surroundings.

Let me explain a little further: I am the youngest of four siblings (one brother and two sisters). Then I decided to live with my father and stepmother, where I became the oldest of five siblings: a stepbrother and three foster sisters. During my life journey, I lived in 4 states with countless addresses, been married, had three children, received an MBA education, traveled all over the US and abroad, and started my own business. Along the way, I was exposed to drugs, alcohol and some levels of physical and mental abuse. I am sure many of you can relate to this and some of you a little more than you would like.

I wish I could tell you that life gets easier as you get older. I wish I could tell you that the responsibilities of being an adult are so much better than being a teenager. Sometimes life is just going to be hard. Some of you may look for ways to numb your pain, anxiety, struggles and heartache to get through these hard times, thinking things will get better or just go away…but the fact is they won't.

I want to offer some hope and encouragement by telling you that your life can be more than what you think it can be. I can tell the positives in your life will far outweigh the negatives. I can tell you that every experience, emotion, and challenge you will face is an opportunity to learn, grow, explore who you are and become better for it. I can tell you all life events are temporary, even the bad ones. Over time, you can learn how to manage change by controlling the things in your life that you are responsible for to help you stay on your path to achieve your goals.

So, what's my point and what does all this have to do with you? More importantly, why should you care? My point is you are just getting started with your life, so don't get discouraged and please don't stop moving on. Some of you may have already experienced enough of life and I am sorry. There is so much to learn, experience and explore in the world - good stuff! That is why you should care.

As a son, brother, stepbrother, foster brother, uncle, teacher, life group leader, mentor and especially a dad, I thought I would share my thoughts and experiences with you through Pivotal Road Life Skills.

Table of Contents

Introduction

Before we get started, I would like to set some expectations for this program. Pivotal Road: Life Skills for Teens was written as my opinions and suggestions for teenagers based on my life experiences as a teenager, brother, father of three, high school substitute teacher, life group leader and mentor. I do not offer or reference expert opinions, studies or statistics. With that said, let's get started, shall we?

I did not realize at the time, but the seed for this program occurred many years ago when I was in college, working full time and helping to raise a family. At that time, life was fulfilling, rewarding and I had an identity and a purpose in life. Let's say life was good! However, I felt I was meant to do something more.

As time passed, opportunities to work with teenagers opened as I became a youth group leader, high school substitute teacher and had an introduction to juvenile facilities. Many teens shared their personal struggles and challenges with life, their homes, identity, relationships and social media.

As I listened to these stories, I wondered how many other teenagers were going through these issues. This really pulled on my heart as it did with my own kids. But what would I say to these kids? What did I have to offer? Then it all started with the questions," If I could go back in time with the knowledge and information as an adult, what would I tell a younger me to help avoid or minimize the bad decisions and mistakes in the future?"

For some of you, life is just starting. For others, life has already begun. I made so many mistakes and bad choices as a teen. I am sure most, if not all, of you have made your share of mistakes too. If you are like me, these mistakes sometimes make you feel vulnerable, inadequate, a failure, fearful, overwhelmed and maybe lonely. However, does a mistake or a couple of them mean your life is over? It may feel like that now, but there is hope.

I have often been told that people are either heading into, in the middle of, or coming out of a life storm or hard season of life. Please take note that these life storms are temporary, and don't last forever, even though it may seem like it. You may not like to hear this, but these storms have a way of shaping your identity based on how you respond during difficult times, what lesson to learn and then applying the lesson to your life. Yes, difficult times teach us about life and about who we are, just as much as the good times. No matter where you are in life, being prepared and having some life tools can make a difference in how well you navigate storms, and may help you become a stronger, more resilient, and confident person.

My goal for you through Pivotal Road is very simple – to provide some guidelines and skills to help you navigate your life storms. This program is not meant to give you all the answers on how to live your life. My hope is you will open your mind and unleash the possibilities for your life, to dream big and set goals for yourself, create a roadmap to move in that direction for a life you dream of, and learn some life skills to work towards achieving your goals. You have value and you can pursue a life that will give you a purpose, direction, and hope for a better future.

PART 1

Life Skills

Life Skill # 1
Communication

Life Skill #1

Communication

Things to think about:

- How you communicate to others says a lot about the type of person you are

- Clear Messaging – Did you really mean to say that?

- Two-Way Communication – Listening is equally as important as speaking.

- Reflection: "My dear brothers and sisters, take note of this: Everyone should be quick to listen, slow to speak and slow to become angry, because human anger does not produce the righteousness that God Desires." James 1:19-20

- Please scan on the QR code to view the video on Communication

There is so much to be said about communication (no pun intended – lol!) and different ways to communicate. I will keep this section to a few recommendations. Let's start with the definition: "It is a process by which information is exchanged between individuals through a common system of symbols, signs, or behavior" – Source Webster-Merriman Dictionary and "the act of communicating with individuals or a message, letter, or announcement" per Cambridge Dictionary.

My children learned to communicate when they were born and so did you. They cried when they wanted something and smiled when they were happy. Eventually, all these sounds became words, and more expressions to communicate our thoughts, ideas, feelings, and emotions with others. Today, there are so many ways to communicate with each other – cell phones, text, emails, social media and even through video games. Just a word of caution – be careful how you communicate. Things can be misunderstood very quickly and can and will get out of hand.

There are two areas of communication I feel we may need a little help with, and they are talking face to face and writing. For instance, my friends and I have our own special way of communicating through words, handshakes, gestures, looks and even writing. But how do I get started meeting someone for the first time? Starting a conversation can be awkward and scary for most people. I found that getting started is half the battle. Once I found something we had in common things got easier. Keep in mind, we won't get along with everyone and that's okay. Just be nice and move on.

As you communicate with others, I highly recommend thinking about the other person as part of your process. Please remember that what you say and how you say it will either inspire and motivate a person or tear them down and create hostility. It really is up to you. A friend once told me to weigh my words carefully, meaning think before I spoke and especially how I would say it.

There is something else I realized that my words are only part of my communication. If I say the same sentence in different tones or volume, I get a completely different response from people. Practice it for yourself with a friend. Say the phrase, "leave me alone" in a nice way and then in a forceful way. Hear the difference? Once you say something, you can't pull it back. It's like trying to put toothpaste back into the tube. Maybe the phrase "words will never hurry me" isn't exactly true.

We all have different ways to express ourselves. That's what makes us who we are. Learning the best way to communicate based on who you are communicating with is a key to your success. My recommendation is simple, learn how to communicate in a way that benefits both you and the person you are speaking to. This will remove any confusion or misunderstandings. As you get older, one of the most important life skills you will need is communication. It is the only way to express yourself to others and especially relationships closest to you.

Take some time for personal reflection and your own personal situations:

- When have you experienced a breakdown in communication in a relationship?

- How did that make you feel? What about the other person?

- What did you learn from that experience and what impact did it have on your life?

- Reflection: James 1:19-20 "My dear brothers and sisters, take note of this: Everyone should be quick to listen, slow to speak and slow to become angry, because human anger does not produce the righteousness that God desires."

Communication Recommendations:

- Conversations: Here are some situations to help you get started.

    o Start with small talk: "Hi, my name is Joe (or Jennifer), how are you? Where do you live? Where did you grow up? What school do you attend?"

    o Moving to personal interests: "What do you like to do for fun? Do you play sports, play or write music, favorite movie, hobbies, draw, paint, etc.? What's your favorite color and why? If you could go anywhere in the world, where would it be and why?"

    o Building a relationship (topics may be more meaningful with depth): "Tell me about your family. Where do they live, and do you get along with them? What is important to you and why?"

- Responses / Non-verbal Communication: if you noticed carefully, sometimes your body responds to support what you are saying or says just the opposite. Here are some key indicators.

    o Voice: How does your voice sound during a conversation? Do you get excited, angry, curious, confused, condescending, scared?

    o Stance: Do you lean towards the person you are talking to that shows you are interested in what they are saying or are you leaning away from them as if not interested?

- o Do you cross your arms, or do you put them on your hips? This may mean you are defensive and don't agree with what the other person is saying. A sign of being relaxed and interested in the conversation is keeping your hands by your side.

  - o Eye Contact: Do you look directly at the other person during the conversation giving them your full attention or do you look away as if not listening at all?

  - o Facial Expressions: Your expressions can sometimes say so much without saying a word. Think about how you feel when someone smiles at you. How about a frown or a mean glare. All are non-verbal communication that can tell you exactly how a person is feeling.

- Writing Skills: This exercise is to help you organize your thoughts as if you are talking to someone. Please don't think of this as homework or an English class assignment. I found that the more I practiced writing down my thoughts and seeing it, then I was able to improve how I communicated with others.

  - o Exercise #1 – choose a topic: write about anything you like such as how to make food, fix something, write a song, play an instrument, some place you'd like to go and what would you do.

  - o Exercise #2 – Think of a person and write a letter to them. It can be about anything. This does not have to be shared with anyone, unless you choose to do so.

- Business Writing Skill: Writing a Resume

  - o A resume is a business tool used to communicate who you are, what type of work you want to do, describes your work experience, skills, training and education to a company. The company reviews this information along with your application to screen through all the other applications to determine who would be a good fit to work at their company.

- o This is your opportunity to show a potential employer why you would be a good hire for their company. From time to time, you may have to update your resume as you learn new skills, get promoted or change jobs to show your professional growth and development. Generally, a resume is required for any interview process, so now would be a good time to start putting one together!

Writing Exercise #1: Choose a Topic & Write About It

Writing Exercise #2 – Write a Letter to Anyone

Phone: 0917 - XXX - XXXX   Email: johndavidalonzo@gmail.com

John David Alonzo
● BS IN INFORMATION AND COMMUNICATIONS ENGINEERING ●

CAREER OBJECTIVE

Seeking a challenging career with a progressive organization that provides an opportunity to capitalize my technical skills & abilities in the field of information technology (IT).

TECHNICAL SKILLS

- Hardware troubleshooting
- Network troubleshooting
- Programming (Java, C++, Visual Basic, Android Programming Language)
- Microsoft Office (MS Word, Excel, Powerpoint, Internet, etc)
- Adobe Creative Suite (Photoshop, InDesign, After Effects, Dreamweaver)

PERSONAL SKILLS

- Excellent written and verbal communication skills
- Highly organized and efficient
- Ability to work independently or as part of a team
- Proven leadership skills and ability to motivate

EDUCATION

BS in Information and Communications Engineering (2010 – 2015)
Rizal Technological University
Boni Avenue, Mandaluyong City

Address

98 Green Meadows Avenue,
Pasig, Philippines

Date of Birth

September 3, 1993

REFERENCES

Available upon request.

ACHIEVEMENTS/ RESPONSIBILITIES

- President, Association of Computer Students
- (2014 - 2015)
- Lay-out Artist, The Guardian Student Magazine (2012 - 2014)
- Vice-Governor, College of Engineering and Industrial Technology (2014 - 2015)

PRE-PROFESSIONAL EXPERIENCE

Technical Support Intern - IT Department
Xerox Business Services Philippines Inc.
(June 2014 – Feb 2015)
Provided Level 1 support, handled troubleshooting and maintenance as well as monitoring and deployment of IT equipment.

Your Resume

Full Name:
Address:
Phone Number:

Statement of Experience / Career Objectives:

Special Skills:

Employment History:

Education Background:

Special Achievements / Honors / Social Clubs

Life Skill # 2
Decision Making

Decision Making

Things to think about:

- How do you make your decisions – based on emotions, facts, or social media?

- Are there any past decisions you would change? Why?

- What are some decisions you are facing now? Do they align with your dreams or goals?

- Reflection: "If any of you lacks wisdom, you should ask God, who gives generously to all without finding fault, and it will be given to you." James 1:5

- Please scan the QR code to view the video on Decision Making

The section is probably the most critical of all. Like communication, making good decisions is a process. My hope during this section is to help you identify how to make the best decisions for your life. Creating this process takes time, trial and error and above all learning from your mistakes in order to make better decisions in the future. For example, think about the last decision you made and what happened afterwards. Did your decision make things better or worse?

I learned that the decisions I made, both good and not so good, had a huge impact on my life. You may have already noticed this in your own journey. I look back at the many Pivotal Roads in my journey and reflect on how my life changed at different points. It did not always work out for the best because I noticed the people that were impacted by my decision. That was not always a positive either. You see, the choices we make don't just affect us. They impact so many other people, especially our families. This made me wonder what the other road would have been like. Maybe some of you can relate.

How do you make your decisions? I feel sometimes we make decisions based purely on emotions and how we feel at that moment and forget about facts. I'm sure you have heard the saying "follow your heart" or maybe "do it if it makes you feel good". However, I caution you in making decisions based on your heart and what feels good. Contrary to this very popular way of thinking, our emotions can and will betray us from doing what feels good over making the right decision. Some of you may have already made decisions based on emotions that did not turn out as well as you had hoped.

So, where am I going with this and what is my point? What I have come to understand is no matter how old you are – having to make tough decisions and choices never go away. In fact, they increase in difficulty as you get older and more complex when more people are involved. Life has a way of forcing us to choose a direction or make a tough decision. Even if we don't decide and try to ignore the circumstance, it is still a decision and could make things worse.

Instead, I recommend implementing some type of safeguard or mechanism to delay making any decisions when you are emotional. For instance, take a deep breath, hold for a few seconds, exhale and ask yourself, "Will this decision help or hurt me and my family? Is it moving me towards my dream or goals?" This simple step really does work, and it has long-term benefits. First, taking this time allows you to control your emotions and not react on impulse that could cause harm and lead to a very poor decision. Another benefit is to engage your mind, to think through your decision, to consider the consequences (good and bad) and to decide the best path for you.

Based on my experiences, making decisions when you are emotional such as stressed, angry, anxious, or feeling pressured isn't the time to make any decision at all and most certainly will not be good sound decisions that are in your best interest. You may end up hurting yourself and the ones you love. Today may be a good time to start changing how you make decisions for the better.

Every day we face choices that force us to make decisions. Each decision creates a ripple effect, positive or negative, that will impact the rest of your life. Even deciding not to do anything is still a decision. Making good decisions acts as the motor that drives you towards the next milestone in achieving your goals. However, during this same time, we are all surrounded by influences that affect our decisions. We have all experienced that soundtrack in our heads from family, friends, music, sports, podcasts, what you read, and especially social media telling us who we are or are supposed to be and how to live our lives. Soon we will have AI (Artificial Intelligence) as an influencer as well.

Outside influences have so much power and impact on your (our) life and our decisions. If we are not careful, they can lead us astray and towards a negative lifestyle. The challenge for you is to learn how to discern or separate the good from the bad. So how do we discern (meaning recognize or identify as separate or distinct – discern right from wrong – source Merriam-Webster) information from these influences to make better choices and decisions for our lives? There are several ways to help build strong discernment skills. One way is to find someone you trust who may be older, wiser, and more experienced in life in making decisions. This could be a family member, a teacher, mentor, older sibling, a Pastor, Life Group Leader, counselor, and the list goes on. I highly suggest you find at least 2 people you trust, have shown good judgement in making decisions, and have your best interests in mind. It would also be wise to find someone who is strong in their faith. Christians are challenged every day, maybe more than others, with temptations and life hardships because of their faith. However, they have also built a relationship with God who provides guidance, direction, and even instructions on how to discern information to make good, positive decisions.

Ask yourself – who do you know that meets these criteria? Do they influence your life to help you or inspire you to make better decisions or do they tempt me and lead in the opposite direction? Where is God in your decision-making process, or is He?

Father God – I pray that You will show up and present Yourself to this person, so they know You are real, alive, trustworthy and You love them unconditionally. Amen.

How Do You Make Decisions Now?

What Would You Change About Decisions from the Past?

What Decisions Are You Facing and How Will You Apply Your New Skills?

Decision #1:

Decision #2:

Decision #3:

Your Resume

Full Name:
Address:
Phone Number:

Statement of Experience / Career Objectives:

Special Skills:

Employment History:

Education Background:

Special Achievements / Honors / Social Clubs

Life Skill # 3
Budgeting / Financial Strategy

Life Skill #3

Budgeting/Financial Strategy

Things to think about:

- What is a budget & why is it important?

- Money Management / Simple Fundamentals: What are your thoughts on money?

- Financial Planning: Do you know where your money goes each month?

- Reflection: *"Do not store up for yourselves treasures on earth, where moths and vermin destroy, and where thieves break in and steal. But store up for yourselves in heaven, where moths and vermin do not destroy, where thieves do not break in and steal. For where your treasure is, there your heart will be also."* Matt 6:19-21

- Please scan the QR code to view the video on Budgeting

Let's talk about money and who does not like money? This is a necessary and important tool in society that we all depend on for our livelihood to pay for food, clothes, housing, transportation - and that's just the basics.

Dave Ramsey, The Total Money Makeover, is quoted as saying "We buy things we don't need with money we don't have to impress people we don't like." – Dave Ramsey, The Total Makeover: A Proven Plan for your Financial Success. I always chuckled at this saying because of the truth behind it.

Let's face it, there is also a negative side to money. We live in a world of the *I want it now* generation. I am just as guilty as the next person with impulse buying, which means buying something on the spot "impulse" without planning and saving for it. Instead, we make the purchase on the spot and usually on credit. My best advice: take caution in this area of your life, be disciplined with your money, and stay out of debt.

Debt is spending more money than you earn and can quickly get out of hand. As mentioned before, avoid this financial trap and be disciplined in your money and learn to make smart purchases. Debt can cause a lot of stress and unnecessary worry in your life. Think of it this way: when you pay high interest rates on credit cards and loans for years, all you are doing is making money for someone else when you could be using that money for you and your family.

Ask yourself, where is my money going? Does it take flight and fly away immediately when I get paid? Who is in control – me or my money?

Strategy / Tactics:

Review the budget template below. It is very important for your future to know how much money you bring home after taxes each month and how much you spend. Next, create your personal budget. Write down your income and all your expenses for the month. Then put your income and expenses in the monthly total spaces below and subtract the two of them. Don't forget to save some of your money too!

- What stood out to you the most? Do you have any money left at the end of the month?

- Is your money working for you or are you working for your money?

- How will this affect your money management planning going forward?

PART 2

Life Plan

Life Skill # 4

You, Your Purpose & Life Mission

You, Your Purpose & Life Mission

Things to think about:

- Who are you? Do you struggle with your identity?

- Who do you want to be? What is your purpose?

- What would you like to do and what is your purpose in life (i.e life mission - dreams, goals) and at what age?

- Reflection: "Trust in the Lord with all your heart and lean not on your own understanding; in all your ways acknowledge Him, and He will make your paths straight." Proverbs 3: 5-6

- Please scan the QR code to view the video on You, Your Purpose and Life Mission

Congratulations! If you are reading this then I am so proud of you for continuing with this program. In this chapter, I am going to challenge you to think deeper and broader about who you are now and the life you would like to have. In the next chapter, you will be given an opportunity to map out a plan and path to achieve it.

One of the hardest things for me was learning who I was as a person and my purpose in life. It took me many years to get answers to these two very important questions. For most of my life, I struggled with mistakes, making poor choices, being very prideful, selfish, and trying to be someone I wasn't meant to be. Basically, I was doing what I thought other people wanted me to do to fit in and be liked only to let myself down continually.

Knowing who I am as a person helps me understand my likes and dislikes, gives me confidence, unable to be easily influenced or offended by other people, able share my opinion in what I believe to be true, and helps me to build healthy relationships with others. Knowing my purpose gives me meaning in life, a reason to live and to stand up for things I truly love and enjoy. It also helped me to realize life is not about me and what I want. I learned my purpose is to serve and help others where needed, which I rely on through my faith. Maybe you have other reasons to learn your identity and purpose.

Don't get me wrong, I have had a pretty good life so far and I still have so much more to do! It just took me a long time to figure things out. Looking back, I wonder what my life would look like if I learned my purpose and mission at an earlier age.

Take a moment, clear your mind and consider your current situation. Be honest with yourself. If you think your life is bad – answer why. And if you think your life is good then do the same thing – answer why.

For Your Consideration:

Ideas for a Purpose:

Example #1: To be the best person I can, love my family and those around me.

Example #2: To experience all that life has to offer, learn from my mistakes to do better and be a positive influence on my family and friends.

Ideas for a Life Mission:

Example #1: I will pursue things that matter to me, share my unique gifts with the world, continually evolve and improve myself, help make the world a better place, foster meaningful relationships, treat time as my most valuable resource, and be grateful everyday I'm alive.

Example #2: To make it through one more day without falling to my temptations, learn to control my anger and bitterness for the world, stop the hatred and rage inside me towards my family and others, foster meaningful relationships starting with my family, help make my world a better place, find value for my life and my time in the world, and be grateful everyday I'm alive.

Describe Who You Think You Are? Who Do You Want to Become?

____

____

____

____

____

____

Life Purpose...

____

____

____

____

____

____

____

____

Life Mission...

____

____

____

____

____

____

____

____

Life Skill # 5
Lifestyle

Lifestyle

Things to think about:

- What lifestyle do you desire?

- Who is influencing the type of lifestyle you seek?

- To consume vs to contribute – which one do you choose?

- Reflection: *"Be very careful, then, how you live – not as unwise but as wise, making the most of every opportunity, because the days are evil."* Ephesians 5: 15-16

- Please scan the QR code to view the video on Lifestle

The goal for this section is to explore the "what-if" scenario to get your mind thinking about the possibilities of achieving the lifestyle you desire. The idea is to create a plan that leads you towards your goal, to become a positive influencer and contributor in society and to the world. In this chapter, I want to challenge you by changing your mindset with this question – what am I willing to do, which may include some uncomfortable decisions, compromises and maybe sacrifices, to achieve my desired lifestyle?

Have you ever thought about the type of lifestyle you wanted to live? I mean really sat and dreamed "BIG" dreams like creating a billion-dollar business, becoming a professional athlete or a world-renowned model or actor, dressing in designer clothes, traveling the world, tasting all kinds of food, meeting different people and exploring cultures? How about a simple life such as living in a small town like I grew up in where everyone knows each other, and the town was your playground?

Let's define "lifestyle" – it is a noun that refers to the way in which a person, group or culture lives. This means there are many sources (some good and not so good) that influence a person's lifestyle, such as family, friends, religious affiliations, social media, magazines, sports, music, the town or city you live in, where you go shopping, and the list goes on.

Over the years, I have realized our lifestyle is determined by our choices. This statement may not be a new concept for many of you. Your choices may have left you feeling out of control or feeling like you have no control in making your own choices. When I was a teenager, many of my important life decisions were made by or discussed with my parents. I realize this may not be an option for most of you. Even with my (divorced) parents' involvement, I did not always make good decisions. As a result, my lifestyle changed a couple times. For instance, I did not have a choice when my mom remarried, and we moved across the country when I was 15. Three months later, I decided to run away and fly back across the country to live with my dad. This one decision completely changed my lifestyle forever. This was a pivotal point in my life because I had the opportunity to live comfortably with my mom vs. experience some economic struggles with my dad.

I believe each person should have the opportunity to set a course towards the type of lifestyle they want to live. I am also not naïve to think I understand your current situation and believe we all come from a family of the rich and famous. Socioeconomic differences are real and generally cause a division between the Have's vs Have Not's, meaning those we feel have everything in life with no struggles and those who struggle daily in life just to find their next meal or even to survive. Take this time to explore your past experiences and see if you can identify the pivotal points that changed your lifestyle.

"Show me your friends, and I'll show you your future." – Gabriel Conte

For Your Consideration:

- What would you do differently in your life if you could choose again?

- How would you use those experiences to make better choices for the lifestyle you desire?

Development Exercise:

What is your current lifestyle today? How does that make you feel?

____

____

____

____

____

____

____

____

____

____

Describe the lifestyle you would like to have - Dream BIG!!!

____

____

____

____

____

____

____

____

____

How would you get started to work towards and achieve your dreams / goals?

____

____

____

____

____

____

____

____

____

____

____

When do you plan to get started? If not now…when?

____

____

____

____

____

____

____

____

____

____

Create Life Plan

Life Skill #6

Create Life Plan

Things to think about:

- What lifestyle do you desire?

- Who is influencing the type of lifestyle you seek?

- To consume vs to contribute – which one do you choose?

- Reflection: *"For I know the plans I have for declares the Lord, plans to prosper you and not harm you, plans to give you hope and a future."* Jeremiah 29:11

- Scan the QR code to view the video on Life Plan

Now it is time to develop your life plan strategy by writing out the steps needed to achieve your goal. To help you on this journey, I recommend creating milestones, or "life-markers", of small steps to accomplish and celebrate along the way to help keep you motivated when things get tough and keep you on track to achieving your goal. Be very specific and detailed in creating the steps to each milestone.

Why is this important? We often get distracted and discouraged in life. The life-marker lets us know we are headed in the right direction. For instance, Life-Marker #1: may require some hard decisions such as remove bad influences – date: now. Life-Marker #2: seek some education, get a job, a place to live – date: 1 year. Life-Marker #3: special training towards your dream / goal – date: 2 years. The point is, each milestone you create should move you towards the next milestone and so on. Start creating your life-markers!

The next step is the execution of your plan. This is where the tire hits the road. Your plan may look good on paper, but until you start living your plan and pursuing your dream, you remain where you are – dreamer of the "what-ifs" instead of moving towards the "what can be"!

You have already written it out in the previous chapters. Now pull all the information together and insert it into the empty spaces provided below. Once you have completed this exercise, read it again. Look at who you described you wanted to be, what you wanted to do and how you plan to achieve this goal. THIS is your Pivotal Road.

Use this time to add more details if needed and be specific with the steps and timelines for your life-markers. This will help you measure your success over time from where you are today. Take note that your current life plan may change during your journey due to unforeseen challenges in life, but that is okay as long as you continue moving towards your goals.

For Your Consideration:

- Who will you share your life plan with for accountability? I suggest you identify 1-2 people you trust to join you on your journey. Give them permission to talk to you openly and honestly to keep you accountable your Pivotal Road.

- Think, focus, create, plan, then execute.

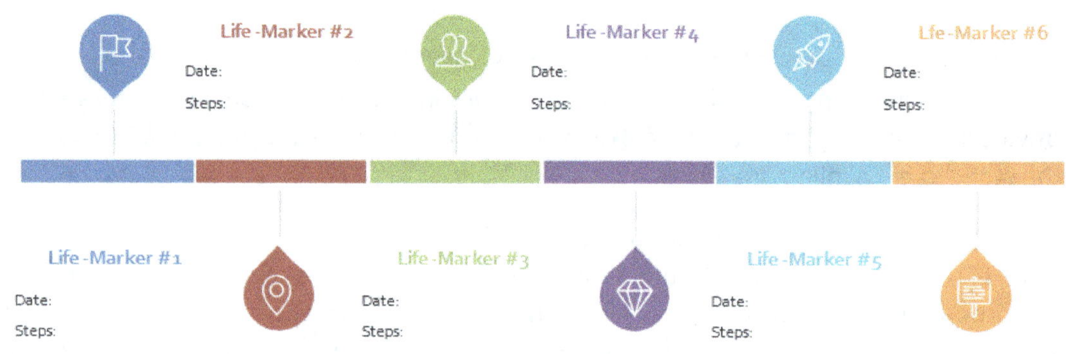

Life-Marker #1:

____

____

____

____

Life-Marker #2:

____

____

____

Life-Marker #3:

____

____

____

Life-Marker #4:

____

____

____

Life-Marker #5:

____

____

____

Life-Marker #6:

____

____

____

Your Life Plan

1) Work on the 3 life skills discussed earlier and apply them into your life.

2) Read your comments in the section "Purpose and Mission". This may change slightly over time as you experience more things in life such as travel, education, family, relationships, careers, heartaches, failures, successes, and so on. The key is to try not to allow too many world influences to determine your identity and purpose. Treat others with respect and dignity even if you don't agree with what they may say or do to you. This is part of your identity is controlling things that ARE in your control – that is you.

3) Review your comments in the section "Lifestyle". Yes, you can achieve these goals and the three life skills – communication, decision making, budgeting – will play a big part in whether you are successful in attaining the lifestyle you desire.

4) Review your comments in the section "Life Plan". The only thing more I can offer is are you ready and willing to execute your plan? If I may offer a couple last pieces of advice; 1) don't talk yourself out of starting to work your plan and 2) don't be afraid of success.

Conclusion - Final Thoughts

Reflection:

- How did it feel to complete a life plan? What did you learn?

- What challenged you the most? How?

- What do you plan to do next?

- God, what are you trying to teach me?

You have reached the end of the Pivotal Road Life Skills for Teens program, but you have also reached a decision for your Pivotal Road to begin your new journey in life.

We are all on a journey through life with a beginning and an ending. What you do between those two life markers is up to you. Your path is determined by the decisions you make (some of you may have lost this option), how you communicate with others, and the money needed to afford and support your goals. I ask that you use these three skills to help you "pivot" away from the current road to a more focused and positive direction.

I do want to offer one word of caution - no plan goes exactly the way you intended. Sometimes detours or "pivots" in life are necessary to change our path to prevent us from getting into trouble or going down the wrong road. This is okay and you should expect detours.

There will be times when you will need to redirect "pivot" your course when facing a life challenge such as a medical emergency, loss of a job, developing an addiction, breakup of a relationship, divorce, miscarriage or a death in the family. These are real life storms that can happen to anyone at any time. These types of events may cause you to slow down or pause your plans and dreams. I ask that you don't get discouraged. Take a deep breath in these moments and think about the recommendations in the sections on communication, decision making and especially your finances before having to make a crucial decision that may have a negative effect on your Pivotal Road.

As you get older and start going through your own life experiences, my hope is that you will review and reflect on what you wrote during this program. These are your words stating your identity, purpose and life plan. The choice now is - do you really want it? Are you ready and willing to execute your life plan? The question for you is - if not now, when?

"God…please use me to further Your kingdom and may You be glorified by my words, actions and deeds…Amen." *A recommended daily prayer by Christopher Terry*